Northborough C.P. School,
Church Street,
Northborough,
Peterborough.

MAPPING ~THE~ UNKNOWN

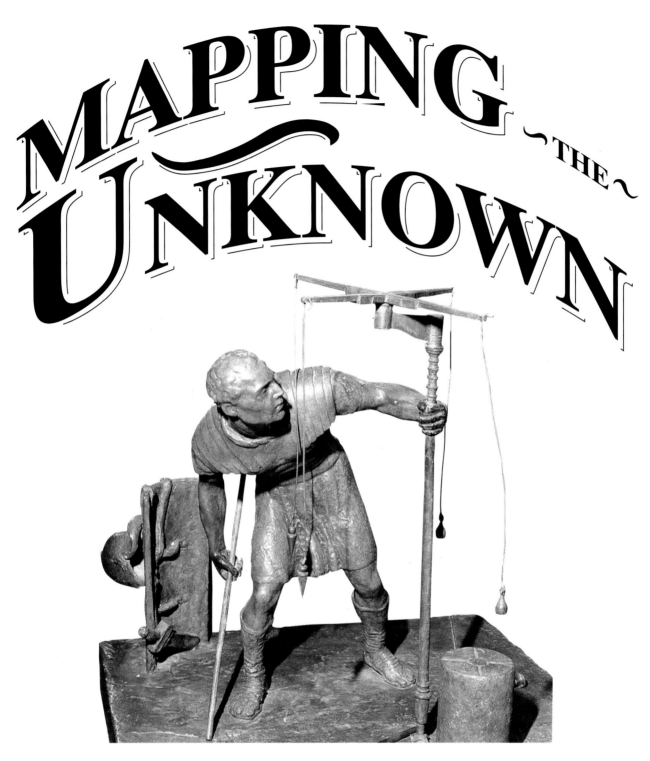

Peter Chrisp

Wayland

Dangerous Waters

MONSTERS OF THE DEEP
PIRATES AND TREASURE
VOYAGES OF EXPLORATION
THE WHALERS

Fearsome Creatures

BIRDS OF PREY
LAND PREDATORS
NIGHT CREATURES
WHEN DINOSAURS RULED THE
EARTH

Frontiers

GREAT JOURNEYS
MAPPING THE UNKNOWN
THE WILD, WILD WEST
THE WORLD'S WILD PLACES

The Earth's Secrets

FOSSILS AND BONES
THE HIDDEN PAST
THE SEARCH FOR RICHES
VOLCANO, EARTHQUAKE AND
HURRICANE

Produced for Wayland (Publishers) Limited by
Roger Coote Publishing
Gissing's Farm, Fressingfield, Eye
Suffolk IP21 5SH, England

First published in 1996 by
Wayland (Publishers) Limited, 61 Western Road
Hove, East Sussex BN3 1JD, England

© Copyright 1996 Wayland (Publishers) Limited

British Library Cataloguing in Publication Data

Chrisp, Peter
   Mapping the Unknown. - (Quest)
   1. Maps - Juvenile Literature
   2. Map drawing - Juvenile Literature
   3. Map reading - Juvenile Literature
   I. Title
   912'.09

   ISBN 0 7502 1384 1

Printed and bound in Italy by
G. Canale & C.S.p.A., Turin

Picture acknowledgements
AKG 17; British Library Reproductions 22-3; CM Dixon *front cover* bottom left, 10t, 20b; ET Archive 7, 15, 39b, 41; Mary Evans Picture Library 5, 11, 21, 31, 32, 38t, 42t; Fotomas Index *front cover,* centre left, 6b, 10b, 20t, 38b; Hulton Deutsch 29t; Image Select 40t/Jacana, 42b; London Transport Museum 24 both; Ministry of Defence (Hydrographic Dept) 6t, 6m; National Maritime Museum, London 4 both; Peter Newark's Pictures 30; Photri 26t; Science Photo Library 12t/European Space Agency, 23b/Bruce Roberts, 26-7/NASA, 27t/NASA Goddard Institute for Space Studies, 28/NASA Goddard Institute for Space Studies, 34/Dr Ken MacDonald, 39t/David Nunuk, 40b/J-L Charmet, 43t, 44-5/NASA; Topham Picturepoint 25; Wayland 9, 16. The artwork is by Peter Bull 7b, 8, 9t, 13, 14, 15t, 16b, 17b, 18, 19, 21t, 25t, 33, 35, 37; Tony Townsend 4l, 12b, 36, 44, and David McAllister *front cover.*

CONTENTS

WHAT IS A MAP?

An impression of one of the Inuit men encountered by Beechey.

Frederick William Beechey

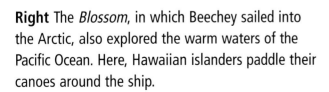

ON a July day in 1826, a small British ship, the *Blossom*, was anchored in Kotzebue Sound, on the coast of what is now Alaska. Its captain, Frederick Beechey, was exploring the coast-line. He went ashore with some of his men to meet the local people, the Inuit, who were standing on the beach.

For both groups, it was a strange meeting. The Inuit were short people dressed in animal skins. Looking up at the tall Englishmen in their blue uniforms, they must have wondered who these strangers could be. For all they knew, the visitors could have come down from outer space. The English also found the Inuit peculiar.

Right The *Blossom*, in which Beechey sailed into the Arctic, also explored the warm waters of the Pacific Ocean. Here, Hawaiian islanders paddle their canoes around the ship.

Beechey wrote that the Inuit women had tattooed chins and that the men's lower lips were pierced and decorated with white lip plugs made of stone.

The two groups quickly made friends and then started trading. The English swapped their tobacco for fish. Beechey even bought some of the stone lip plugs worn by the men. They were happy to take these out, leaving big holes in their lower lips. Some of the sailors were shocked at the sight of these holes. The Inuit thought this was a great joke. Beechey wrote that they laughed at the sailors, *'thrusting their tongues through the holes, and winking their eyes.'*

Lines in the sand

Although the two groups seemed to come from very different worlds, they were able to make themselves understood by using sign language. Beechey wanted to find out as much as he could about the area. Soon, the Inuit were bending down and making marks in the sand. Beechey wrote: *'The coastline was first marked out with a stick, and the distances [were] regulated by the day's journeys.*

Sir John Ross and his men meet an Inuit tribe. Early Arctic explorers were sometimes uncertain what was ice and what was solid ground, which made mapping the region very difficult.

Beechey's map of Kotzebue Sound. The dots in the sea show where Beechey took measurements of the depth of water.

The hills and ranges of mountains were next shown by elevations of sand or stone, and the islands represented by heaps of stones, their proportions being duly attended to. The villages and fishing stations were marked by a number of sticks placed upright. In time, we had a complete topographical plan of the coast from Point Darby to Cape Kruzenstern.'

The Inuit had made a map, a special kind of picture made to help us understand our world. Beechey's description of it tells us a lot about what maps are and how they work.

Below Beechey made sketches of the coast around Kotzebue Sound. They showed the cliffs, bays and beaches that would help other mariners who visited the area to work out where they were.

Below This map, drawn in the thirteenth century, is based on a Roman road map. The mapmaker was more concerned with showing which roads led where than with accurately portraying hills, rivers and so on.

Choosing what to show

The Inuit map was a simplified picture of the coast, as if seen from high up in the air. Like all maps, it could only show a limited amount of information. Mapmakers have to choose the things that are important to them. The Inuit chose to include their villages and the places where they fished.

When Beechey drew his own map of Kotzebue Sound, he chose different information – the sorts of things that would be useful to a ship's captain. He ignored the villages and fishing places. To Beechey, these were unimportant. But he included the depth of the sea at various points around the coast. This didn't matter to the Inuit because they used light, shallow boats.

Different maps serve different purposes. You can see this if you compare an area of a country on a road map with the same area on a map designed for walkers. The road map doesn't show hills or valleys, but the walkers' map does.

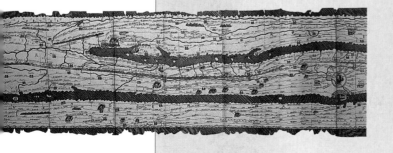

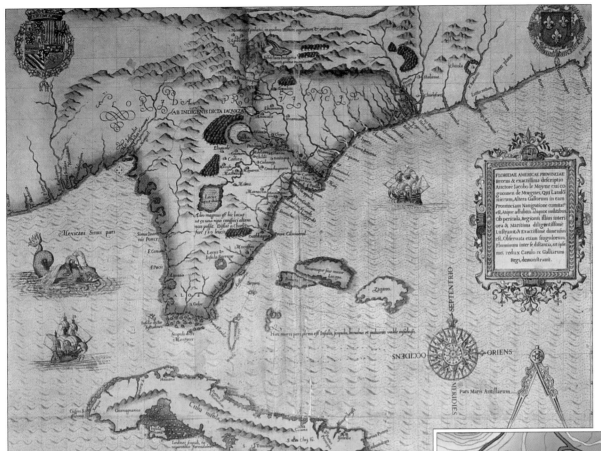

Below It is much easier for us to recognize hills on a map if they are shaded. The shading is always drawn as if the sun is shining from the north-west. If the hills were shaded as if the sun were to the south-east, our eyes would read them as hollows instead of hills.

A map of Cuba and the south-east of North America, drawn in 1591. The artist has shown a line of hills simply by drawing a picture of them on his map, which is clear but not very accurate. The sea is shown using small, shaded-in waves.

Drawing the shape of the land

Beechey called the Inuit map a 'topographical plan'. This means that it was a map showing the features of the landscape, such as hills. It was easy for the Inuit to show hills because their map was also a model. They could make tiny hills out of sand. But how do you show a hill on a flat piece of paper?

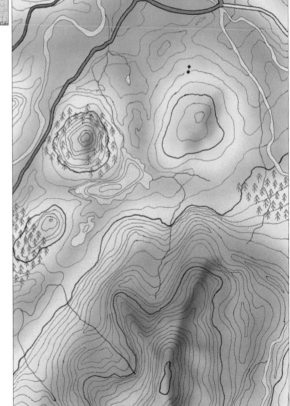

M5 Motorway, with service area	**Garden**
Woodland	**Site of battle**
Slope	**Wildlife park**
Beach	**Information centre**
Airport	**Golf course**
Castle	**Camping/ caravanning site**

Symbols

The Inuit map used symbols – signs or pictures that stand for things in the real world. The Inuit symbols were sticks, which stood for their villages and the places they fished. Our maps use symbols, too. For example, a picture of an elephant might stand for a zoo, or a flag for a golf course.

Maps use symbols, colours, shading and lines in order to give us information. In order to read a map, you need to understand what all these different things mean. You have to know that the colour blue means water, and that an elephant stands for a zoo, and not for a herd of wild elephants.

Maps show hills in various ways. One method is to use contour lines. These are imaginary lines joining together areas that are the same height above sea level. On a gentle slope, the lines are far apart. On a steep hillside, they are close together. With contour lines, you can show the shape of a hill with great accuracy. The only problem is that it doesn't look much like a hill.

Contour lines are easier to understand if the spaces between them are given different colours. Low-lying areas sometimes have a light colour, such as pale green. Higher areas are shown by shades of brown.

The best way of making a hill really look like a hill is to use shading. One side of the hill is slightly darkened as if the sun is shining on it from the north-west. Modern maps may combine shading with contour lines.

Drawing to scale

Most maps are drawn to scale. Small distances on the map stand for much bigger distances in the real world. For example, a centimetre on a map might show a real distance of 1,000,000 cm (10 km) – this is a scale of 1:1,000,000. The amount of detail a map can show depends on the scale chosen by the map-maker.

The Inuit were not able to measure distances accurately, but their map was drawn to a sort of scale. They measured distances by how long it took to travel them. On their map, part of the coast which took two days to travel along was drawn twice as big as part which took one day.

An ancient Islamic map of the world. At the centre of the map lies the Kaaba Mosque in the Holy City of Mecca. On a map such as this, scale is not important – the map's purpose is to show the Kaaba at the heart of Islam.

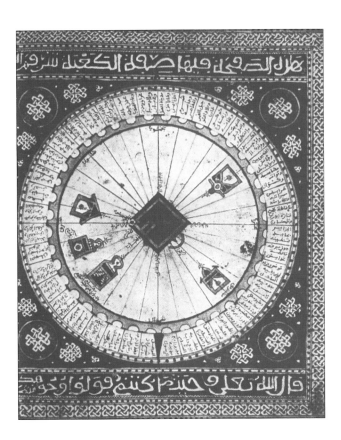

Different types of map are drawn for different purposes. The map at the top of the page shows roads, towns and places of interest, such as the castle. It would be useful to motorists. The map below it, with contours, slopes, woodlands and footpaths, is designed for walkers.

WHAT SHAPE IS OUR WORLD?

THE oldest belief about the shape of the Earth, first recorded around 5,000 years ago, is that it is flat. There are still people who think that we live on a flat Earth. In 1994, the Flat Earth Research Society International, based in California, USA, had 2,800 members. This is how the 'Flat Earthers' describe their beliefs:

'Members rely only on 'provable' knowledge and consequently believe that the 'spinning ball' theory regarding the Earth is absurd, and that, in reality, the Earth is flat and infinite (endless) in size. Members maintain that Australia is not under the world, Australians do not hang by their feet, head down, nor do ships sail over the edge of the world to get there.'

The Society publishes *Flat Earth News*, which is full of articles attacking modern science for giving a false view of the world. However, most people today believe that the Earth is spherical, not flat.

This group of people are standing by their apparatus for trying to prove that the earth is flat.

This ancient Babylonian map of the known world shows Babylon at the centre. Many maps show the homes of the original map-makers in the centre – most modern world maps were originally drawn by Europeans, and show Europe in the middle.

Mapping the Earth's insides

On 10 April 1818, an American ex-soldier called Captain John Cleves Symmes sent a letter to the world's most famous scientists and to the US government. He wrote:

'To All The World: I declare that the Earth is hollow and habitable within... and that it is open at the poles... I pledge my life in support of this truth and am ready to explore the hollow, if the World will support and aid me in the undertaking.

I ask a hundred brave companions well equipped to start from Siberia, in the fall season, with reindeer and sleighs on the ice of the frozen sea. I engage that we will find a warm and rich land, stocked with thrifty vegetables and animals, if not men... We will return the succeeding spring.'

Symmes was hurt and disappointed by the reaction to his letter. Instead of offering help with the expedition, people laughed at him. He spent the rest of his life trying to convince people that the Earth was hollow. But he was never able to set off in search of 'Symmes' hole', as the imaginary opening at the North Pole came to be called.

Symmes' son, Americus, was one of the few people who believed in his hollow Earth idea. Americus Symmes

argued that the Earth must be hollow because God would have made it that way. A solid Earth would be pointless and wasteful. But a hollow Earth, which you could live inside, 'would result in a great saving of stuff.'

Captain John Cleves Symmes, the American hollow-earth theorist.

How do we know that the Earth is a ball?

We have seen photographs of our planet taken from space. It looks like a big, coloured ball, hanging in the blackness. Flat Earthers think that these photos are fakes. But even without the photos, we have good reasons for believing that we live on a big ball.

The arguments for a ball-shaped Earth were first written down over two thousand years ago, by the ancient Greeks. They worked out that the Earth was round simply by using their eyes. Here are some of their arguments.

Imagine that you are at the top of a tower on the coast, watching a boat sail out to sea. If our world was flat, you would expect the boat to get smaller and smaller. Eventually, it would be just a tiny dot and then it would vanish. But in fact, a boat does not disappear like this. First, its hull vanishes beyond the horizon and then its mast. This shows that the sea must have a curved surface.

A view of the earth from space taken by the Meteosat weather satellite.

If you were watching a ship sail out to sea, at first (**A**) you would be able to see all of it (above the waterline). But as it passed over the horizon it would begin to disappear (**B**) and finally would vanish from sight completely (**C**).

In about 230 BC, the Greek mathematician Eratosthenes measured the size of the Earth. He knew that on 21 June every year, the Sun's rays shone directly down a well at Syene, Egypt. At the same time, the angle of a shadow cast by a vertical column at Alexandria was 7.2° – one-fiftieth of a circle's 360°. So the distance from Syene to Alexandria was one-fiftieth of the way around the Earth. The two places were about 780 km apart, so the Earth was 50 times that, or 39,000 km, in circumference. He wasn't far out; the true figure is just over 40,000 km.

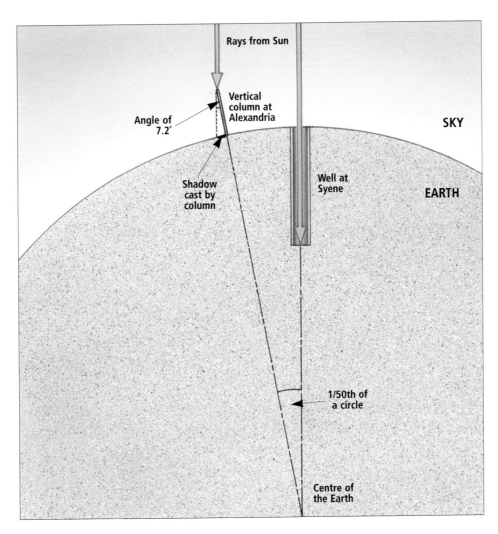

The Greeks also noticed that the sky looks different from different places. If you travel north, for example, new stars come into view which can't be seen further south. The sun also appears at different heights in the sky depending on how far north or south you are. This could only happen if we were moving around the surface of a ball-shaped Earth. From a flat Earth, the stars and the sun would appear in the same place, no matter where you were.

THE WHOLE WORLD ON A MAP

THE trouble with living on the surface of a ball is that it has no beginning and no end. This makes it difficult to say where any one place is in relation to other places. Suppose you were a sailor on a yacht, sinking in the middle of the ocean. You could send a radio message asking for help. But how could you tell your rescuers where to find you?

Map-makers solved this problem by drawing imaginary lines around the Earth. These include the equator – a line going from east to west around the middle of the Earth – and, above and below it, horizontal lines of latitude, or parallels.

Lines of longitude, or meridians, run vertically from north to south. The 0° meridian, which passes through Greenwich, England, is the most important; all of the others are measured in degrees east or west of it. In the same way, lines of latitude are measured in degrees north or south of the 0° parallel, which is the Equator.

Lines of longitude and latitude.

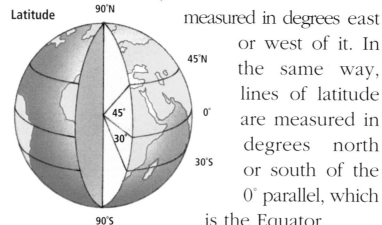

The world turned upside down?

In 1979 an Australian, Stuart McArthur, produced a map rather like the one shown here. Does anything about it strike you as peculiar? McArthur explained what he was doing in the map's caption:

'At last, the first move has been made – the first step in the long-overdue crusade to elevate (raise) our glorious but neglected nation… to its rightful position – towering over its Northern neighbours… Never again to suffer the perpetual onslaught of 'down under' jokes… Finally South emerges on top.

So spread the word. Spread the map!

South is superior. South dominates!

Long live AUSTRALIA – RULER OF THE UNIVERSE!'

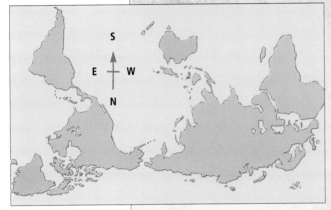

A version of Stuart McArthur's 'Universal Corrective Map of the World'.

McArthur's map looks upside down. But since the Earth is ball-shaped, there is no such thing as a 'right way up' on a map. It is only because we are used to maps showing north at the top that this one looks funny. In fact, six hundred years ago, European maps often had east at the top.

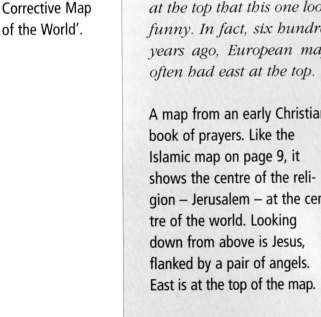

A map from an early Christian book of prayers. Like the Islamic map on page 9, it shows the centre of the religion – Jerusalem – at the centre of the world. Looking down from above is Jesus, flanked by a pair of angels. East is at the top of the map.

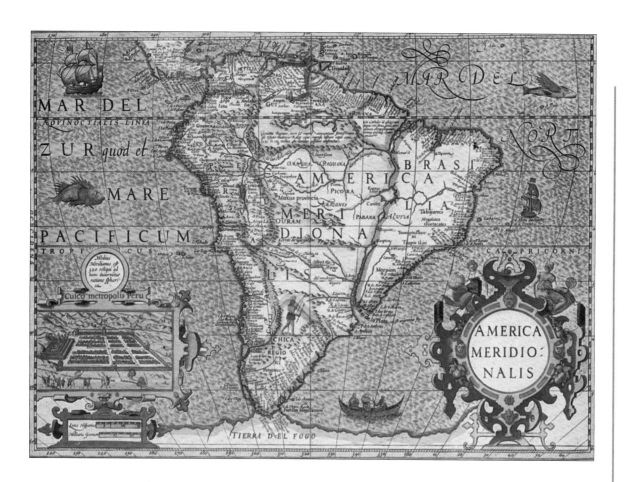

South America, from Gerhard Mercator's *Atlas*. Mercator lived from 1512–1594; the edition of the *Atlas* this map comes from was published in Antwerp, The Netherlands, in 1633. Most modern atlases still use Mercator's method of flattening out the globe.

Every place on Earth can be described by its latitude and longitude. Sydney, Australia, for example, is 33.55 degrees south of the equator and 151.10 degrees east of the Greenwich meridian. In the index of an atlas, this appears as Latitude 33.55°S and Longitude 151.10°E. Look up the place where you live in the index of a large atlas. You will find its latitude and longitude.

Flattening the Earth

Map-makers who want to show the whole world have one big problem: maps are flat, but the world is round. In order

Most map projections are based on either a cylinder, a cone or a plane (flat surface).

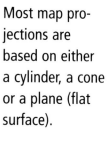
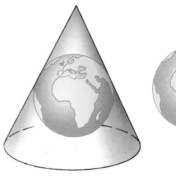

16

Gerhard Mercator (on the left) with fellow map-maker Jodocus Hondius. They are measuring out distances on the globe, in preparation for transferring them on to the page. Mercator died before his *Atlas* could be completed, and it was Hondius who added the maps that made up the finished *Atlas*.

to show our round world on a flat surface, map-makers have to twist the truth. They have to bend, squeeze or stretch countries or areas of sea to fit them on to the paper.

There are many different ways of doing this, called map projections. All of them change the shape of the world in one way or another. Some alter the shape of countries, others their size or the distance between them.

The best-known map projection was invented in the 1560s by a Dutch map-maker called Gerhard Mercator. It is called a cylindrical (tube-shaped) projection. It is as if Mercator has wrapped a tube of paper around a glass globe with a light inside it. The light has thrown the shapes of countries on to the paper. The shapes have been traced on to the paper, and the paper unrolled.

On a globe, lines of longitude curve inwards, meeting at the poles.

This illustration shows how lines of latitude and longitude are projected on to a sheet of paper in Mercator's projection. This results in areas at the far north and south of the globe becoming very distorted.

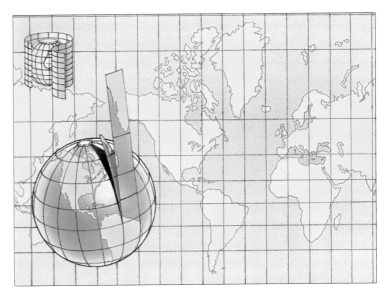

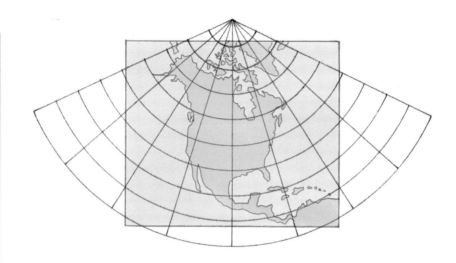

In a conical projection, the lines of longitude and latitude are projected on to a paper cone wrapped around a globe. The lines of longitude appear to radiate straight out from the poles, while the lines of latitude are concentric circles around the poles.

But on Mercator's map, these lines are parallel. By drawing them like this, Mercator has stretched the areas of the Earth nearest to the poles. As a result, the lands at the top and bottom of the map look much bigger than they really are. Greenland, for example, looks enormous on Mercator's map. In fact, it is eight times smaller than South America.

Mercator knew that his map made countries look the wrong size. This didn't bother him because his map was invented for a special purpose. It was meant for sailors, who need to know the true direction of one place from another. For a sailor who has to plan a route, knowing the direction of a country is more important than knowing its size.

There are a number of different projections that can be used to show the whole world on a flat piece of paper. A few of them are shown here.

Mollweide's projection

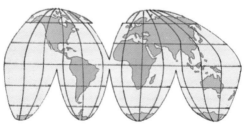

Goode's interrupted projection

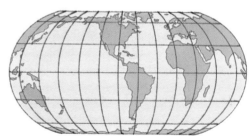

Eckert's projection

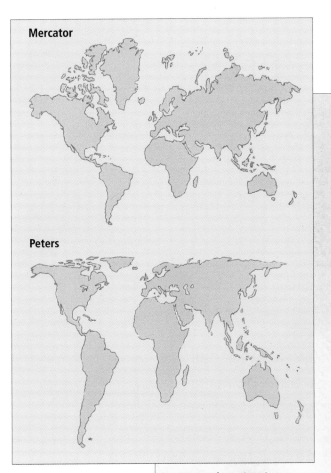

Mercator

Peters

Peters' projection produces a very different map from the more commonly used Mercator's projection.

An unfair map?

People have complained that Mercator's map gives an unfair picture of the world. It makes North America and Europe, the richest parts of the world, look big. Meanwhile poorer places, such as Africa and South America, have been shrunk. On Mercator's map, poor countries seem less important than rich countries.

This world map was drawn by a German historian called Arno Peters. He said that it was 'based on the equal status of all peoples'. He took Mercator's map, stretched the countries in the middle, and squashed those at the top. Peters' map shows the true sizes of different lands. But it does so by bending their shapes.

An American map-maker, Arthur Robinson, complained that this was like looking at the world in a trick mirror at a fairground. He wrote that Peters had made the land masses look 'like wet, ragged, long winter underwear hung out to dry'. Robinson hated Peters' map because he thought it looked strange.

Although Mercator's map was specially designed for sailors, it began to be used for lots of other purposes. Today it is the most familiar picture of the world. This is partly because of its shape. Unlike many other projections, it is rectangular – the right shape for the page of a book, a wall poster or a TV screen.

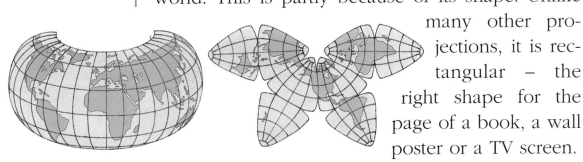

Armadillo projection

Cahill's butterfly projection

MAPPING THE LAND

EVERY summer between 1555 and 1561, a young man could be seen riding on horseback through Bavaria in Germany. To the local villagers, his behaviour must have seemed very peculiar. He seemed to be drawn towards church towers and hilltops. At each village he reached, he would climb to the highest point, usually a church tower. Then he would take out a strange-looking device and fiddle with it. Having written something in a notebook, he would then ride off. Who was he, and what on Earth was he doing?

The young man's name was Philip Apian, and he was making a map. He liked to keep his methods secret, in case rival map-makers found out about

A Roman soldier uses a complicated system of weights and balances to survey the land ahead. He was probably part of a road-building team, trying to find the most direct route.

Philip Apian in the Bavarian countryside. Instead of the guns the two figures in the background are carrying, he has with him his secret triangulation device.

This woodcut shows a group of Arab astronomers in the sixteenth century. The man in the centre is measuring angles with an instrument called a diopter. Apian would have used a similar device to make his maps of Bavaria.

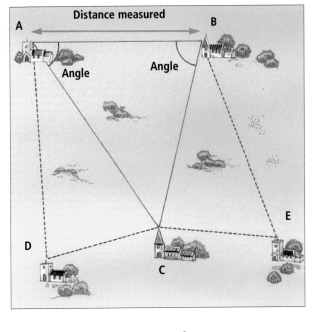

Distance measured

A

Angle

B

Angle

E

D

C

them. But, thanks to his notes, we have a good idea of what he was up to. These notes are mostly names of places and lists of angles. This was what he was doing up the church towers: he was measuring angles.

Apian was using a new method of map-making, called triangulation. This is a way of finding out the position of different places by joining them up to form imaginary triangles. Triangles have a useful feature: if you know the length of one side and the angles at each end, you can work out the lengths of the other two sides without having to measure them.

Apian's surveying technique. First he measured the distance between two church towers (**A** and **B**). This was the first side of a triangle. From the top of each tower he measured the angle of a third tower (**C**). This made up a triangle, and Apian could work out the lengths of its other sides (**A-C** and **B-C**) without measuring them. He then made other triangles using other towers (**D** and **E**).

TERRÆ·MO··TVS

The earliest picture of a European map-maker at work, from the *Methodus Geometrica* of 1598. Apian's map had been published 30 years before this woodcut appeared: if you compare the quality of his map, shown on the right, you can see how skilful it was.

Below A copy of one of Philip Apian's finished maps. On it, you can see many of the church towers he climbed to take measurements of angles he needed for the map.

Apian spent six summers travelling from village to village, covering the whole of Bavaria with imaginary triangles. In the winter months, it was too cold to be up church towers. He spent this part of the year at home in Munich, using his notes to draw an enormous map. Eventually, the whole thing measured 42 square metres.

This map has been lost. But a much smaller version was published in 1568, as a 24-page atlas entitled *Maps of Bavaria*. Every detail in it had to be carved by hand on blocks of wood, which were then used for printing.

Map-making today

Map-making has changed in many ways since Philip Apian was riding around Bavaria. He had to do everything himself, from taking measurements to drawing his map. Nowadays, the different jobs are done by specialists.

The people who do the measuring are called surveyors. They still take sightings from high points, such as hilltops and church towers, and they also plot imaginary triangles. But, unlike Apian, they can measure distances just as quickly as angles.

A modern surveyor takes a measurement using a theodolyte, a laser instrument which uses the same principles as Apian's triangulation device did, almost 400 years ago.

Mapping the Underground

Deep below the streets of London, England, trains are moving through tunnels. Every day, two and a half million people travel around the city using the 'Underground'. It is a complicated system, with several different lines. Passengers may have to change trains two or three times before they reach their destination. In order to know where to change from one line to another, they need a good, simple map.

Early maps of the London Underground showed what the lines would look like from above, if you could peel off the surface of the city and look underneath. In the busy central area, there are many stations close together. Away from the centre, the stations get more and more spread out. These maps were not very easy to use.

In 1931, a young draughtsman, Henry Beck, decided to redesign the map and make a version that people could use. Beck realized that when you're on a train, it doesn't matter whether you're travelling in a curve or a straight line. You don't need to know your exact location. All you have to know is that you're heading for the right station. So he straightened out all the lines,

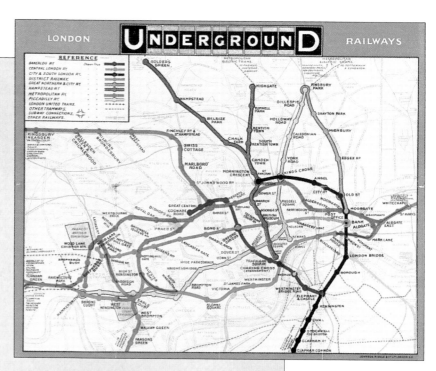

Above A map of the London Underground, from 1908.

ignoring their real shapes.

As well as ignoring real shapes, Beck's map ignores distances. The busy central area has been stretched, to give more space for the stations. Meanwhile, the outer area has been shrunk, so that more of its stations can be included. At last, you can see the whole train system and you can make sense of it.

In 1933, Beck's map was displayed in every Underground station in London. It has been in use ever since, although it has been updated many times. Today, maps like Henry Beck's are used all over the world, by bus companies, railways and airlines.

Above A map of the London Underground, from 1908.

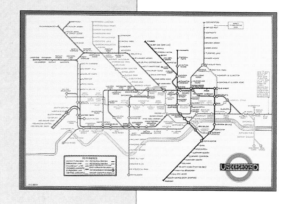

Henry Beck's revolutionary map of 1933.

They do this with electronic equipment which uses radio or sound waves, or light rays.

Apian could only map places that he could see clearly and reach on horseback. We can tell from his map that he usually stayed in the valleys. Mountains and forests were difficult for him to reach and survey, and they are not shown very accurately on his map.

Nowadays, we can map places that are almost impossible to reach, thanks to aeroplanes and photography. A plane can fly over mountains, jungles or polar ice, taking a series of overlapping photographs. These photographs can then be converted by a computer into a map.

Area covered by one photograph

Taking aerial photographs for map-making. Photographs are taken one after another, and each one slightly overlaps the last so that no detail is lost.

This man is making a map using measurements taken from aerial photographs. This process is called photogrammetry.

Mapping from space

Space flight has had an enormous effect on map-making. Satellites, circling hundreds of kilometres above our heads, are constantly photographing the planet. It took Philip Apian six years to finish his survey of Bavaria. A modern satellite can photograph the entire surface of the Earth in 18 days.

Left A photograph of Italy, Sicily, Sardinia and Corsica, taken by the Landsat satellite. If you compare it to a map, you will be able to see whether the map projection is accurate or not.

Satellites can also photograph a small area of the planet over a long period of time. In this way, we can see forests getting smaller, as they are chopped down. We can see cities and deserts gradually growing bigger. Apian could only map fixed landmarks. Our modern maps can show the way the world is changing.

Thanks to computers, today's maps don't even have to keep still. On a screen, you can zoom in and out of a map. You can move from looking at a whole country to a town. You can follow weather systems, such as hurricanes, as they make their way across the oceans. Apian would he amazed by the maps we use today!

A satellite weather map of the spiral of clouds around Hurricane Florence in 1994. You can see the small, clear eye of the storm in the centre.

This computer-generated map of the past shows what scientists think the world's vegetation was like 18,000 years ago, during the last Ice Age. The area that is now the Sahara desert was then grassland.

THE EARTH'S HIDDEN LANDSCAPES

This computer-generated map shows the high mountains on land and the depths of the oceans. The mountains are shown in pale yellow or white, while the ocean deeps show as pink.

FOR thousands of years, people have been terrified of earthquakes. They have come up with many different explanations for them. The ancient Greeks believed that they were caused by the sea god, Poseidon, whom they called the 'Earth-shaker'. The Japanese blamed the wriggling of a giant catfish which lived deep underground.

Earthquake zones

Most earthquakes happen under the sea, and they are more common in certain places than in others.

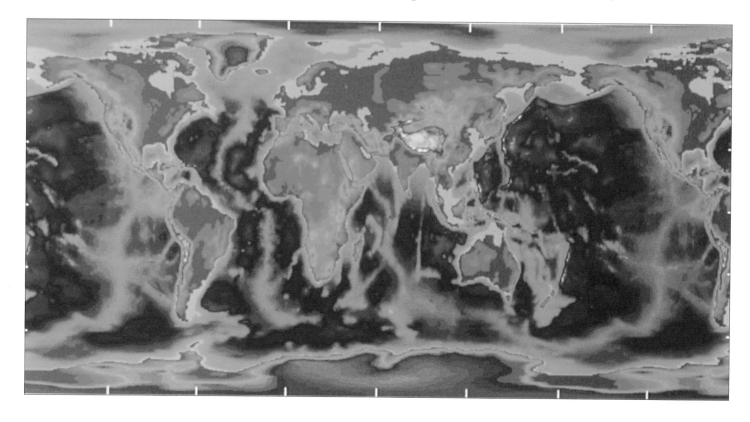

Earthquake!

At just after three o'clock in the morning, on 4 February 1976, strange things started happening all over Guatemala, in Central America. People were woken by odd noises. They saw lamps above their heads swinging from side to side. Cups started rattling and falling off shelves.

Near the south coast, a farmer, looking out of his window, was amazed to see the water in his swimming pool splashing all by itself. At Tikal in the north, a sleeping tourist was woken by a thudding sound. At first, he thought it was his room-mate stomping around. Then he realized it was something much more serious: 'I didn't know it was an earthquake until I heard the monkeys and parrots in the jungle. They raised a terrible racket.'

Guatemala had been hit by a huge earthquake. The first shock lasted just thirty seconds, but it could be felt over a huge area, from the Atlantic to the Pacific. There was terrible damage, especially in the capital, Guatemala City. Whole streets were ripped apart. Buildings crashed to the ground, burying thousands of people in the rubble. More shocks followed over the next few days. By the end, around 23,000 people had been killed and 77,000 injured. More than a million people lost their homes.

Devastation in Guatemala City in the aftermath of the 1976 earthquake, which measured 7.5 on the Richter scale. The quake caused damage estimated to have cost six billion US dollars, and claimed thousands of lives.

They happen in particular around the edges of the Pacific Ocean, from New Zealand up to Japan and down the west coast of North and South America – an area nicknamed the 'ring of fire'. Another zone of frequent earthquakes stretches east from the Mediterranean Sea.

By looking under the sea, and drawing maps of the bottom, scientists have discovered the true cause of earthquakes. At the same time, they made some amazing discoveries about our planet.

Running along with a heavy sea behind it, HMS *Challenger* begins the first world-wide oceanographic survey in 1872.

30

Mapping the sea bed

Oceans cover more than seven-tenths of our planet's surface. Yet, until very recently, we knew very little about them. We didn't know how deep they were or how far down life could be found. We had no idea of the shape of the sea bed.

Undersea mapping really began on 7 December 1872, when a British Royal Navy ship called HMS *Challenger* set off on a three-and-a-half-

year voyage around the world. The *Challenger* was a warship that had been converted into a scientific laboratory. It carried hundreds of bottles for taking samples of sea water; weighted ropes for measuring the depth of the sea; and nets for scooping up animals and plants.

As it travelled around the world, the *Challenger* had to make regular 'stations', or stops. At each one, the depth of the sea was measured and samples of water, animals and mud were collected from the bottom.

After two years at sea, the survey continues. Here the crew of the *Challenger* are collecting samples of water and creatures from the depths. They have hauled the container up by hand.

31

Scientists aboard the *Challenger* at work in the ship's laboratory. Hanging by the neck in the background are unusual birds the crew has caught; the scientists are using microscopes and measuring instruments to examine their finds.

The *Challenger* made many discoveries about the sea. Hundreds of strange-looking creatures were dragged up and examined. There were fish with huge eyes, suited to living in the blackness of the deep ocean. Other fish had no eyes at all. The scientists also found some unusual features of the sea bed. Near the Mariana Islands, in the Pacific, they measured a depth of 8,184 m. This was the Marianas Trench, where the sea is deeper than anywhere else in the world. They also found a bump in the middle of the Atlantic. It was a chain of mountains, which was named the Mid-Atlantic Ridge.

Mapping with sound

In the 1920s, scientists invented a much quicker way to map the sea bed using sound waves – called echo sounding. An electrical device on board a ship makes a sharp 'ping' noise. This travels down through the water, hits the sea bed and then bounces back as an echo. By measuring the time it takes to return, scientists can work out the depth of the water. Using echo sounding, a ship can get a continuous picture of the sea floor below.

Using sound waves to map the sea bed. This technique can also be used to locate objects such as shipwrecks on the sea bed, and can even enable fishermen to detect large shoals of fish.

Image of shipwreck and fish shoal on sonar screen

Wave reflected back

Sound wave

Fish shoal

Shipwreck

Sea bed

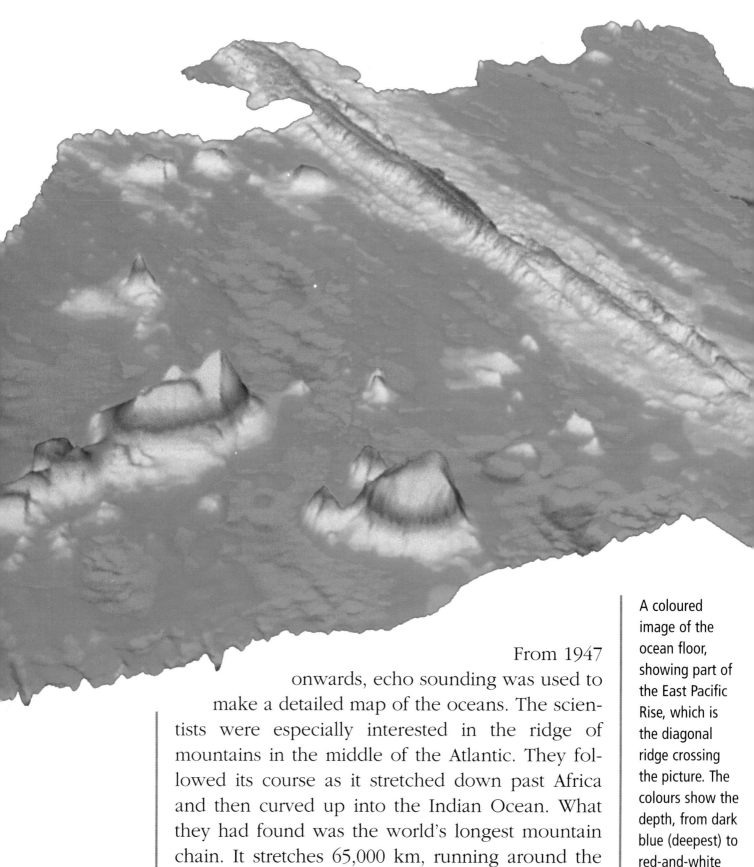

From 1947 onwards, echo sounding was used to make a detailed map of the oceans. The scientists were especially interested in the ridge of mountains in the middle of the Atlantic. They followed its course as it stretched down past Africa and then curved up into the Indian Ocean. What they had found was the world's longest mountain chain. It stretches 65,000 km, running around the Earth like the seam on a leather ball.

A coloured image of the ocean floor, showing part of the East Pacific Rise, which is the diagonal ridge crossing the picture. The colours show the depth, from dark blue (deepest) to red-and-white (shallowest).

Sound was also used to map the Marianas Trench in the Pacific, which was found to be 11,033 m at its deepest point. More deep trenches were found, curving around the western Pacific.

Scientists soon noticed that there was a link between the features of the sea bed and earthquakes. On a map, they could see that areas where earthquakes were known to take place, such as the 'ring of fire' around the Pacific, were in the same places as the sea's mountains and trenches. It took a while to understand just why this was.

The continents are moving

In 1912, a German scientist called Alfred Wegener put forward the idea that millions of years ago all the Earth's continents, or landmasses, were joined together and surrounded by sea. He had noticed that the coastlines of different continents fitted each other like pieces in a jigsaw puzzle. If you look at the coasts of South America and Africa, you can see this for yourself.

Wegener suggested that somehow, over a very long period, the continents had drifted apart. At the time, most scientists laughed at his idea. How could the continents have moved?

The locations of earthquakes and volcanoes often match up with the positions of undersea ridges and deep ocean trenches.

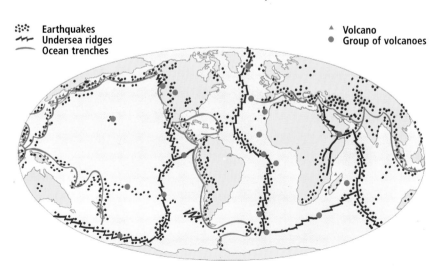

::: Earthquakes
〜 Undersea ridges
— Ocean trenches

▲ Volcano
● Group of volcanoes

The sea bed provided the answer. Scientists now believe that our earth's crust, or surface, is made up of more than a dozen huge 'plates', or slabs. These plates rest on top of hot, liquid rock, like rafts floating on water.

The trenches and mountains under the sea make up some of the edges of the plates. Other edges can be found on land, in places like Guatemala. Here, two plates – the American and the Caribbean – are pushing against each other.

At the great mountain ridges in the middle of seas, hot rock is constantly being forced up from below, and it cools and hardens to form the ridges. At the same time, this newly formed rock pushes against the plates on either side. This is the force that is moving the continents around the Earth. It is making the Atlantic Ocean grow by about 5 cm a year.

At an ocean trench, the opposite is happening. There a plate is being pushed back down into the Earth, where it melts, and rejoins the liquid rock.

Where plates move apart, new land is made when molten rock rises to the surface and cools.

Where plates are moving towards each other, one is forced down below the other. Many earthquakes occur at such plate boundaries.

A map of the future

Scientists have worked out the speed and direction of movement of the landmasses. They believe that 50 million years from now, Australia will have travelled north towards Asia; a chunk of Africa will have split away; and North and South America will have moved apart. With this in mind, they have drawn a map of our world in the distant future.

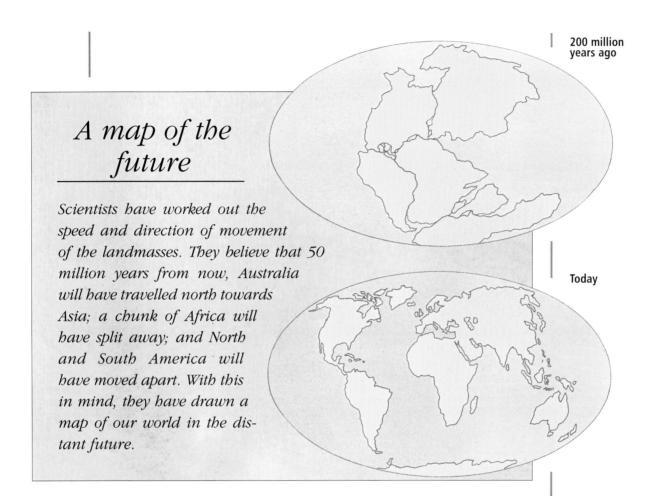

200 million years ago

Today

50 million years from now

Where two plates are pushing against each other, enormous forces build up. Eventually, the rock just gives way and the result is an earthquake. This is what happened in Guatemala in February 1976. The northern plate made a sudden lurch of 1.5 m, tearing the country in two.

A MAP OF THE NIGHT SKY

This map of the night sky shows all the constellations and the things they were named for. Can you spot the Great Bear, Scorpio and the twins of Gemini among the others?

OVER two thousand years ago, ancient Greek myths told a story about a great hunter called Orion. He was a giant, so tall that he could wade across the sea without getting his head wet. Dressed in a golden breastplate, Orion would stride from island to island, flattening animals with a huge club. Nothing was strong or fast enough to escape him. Orion boasted

that he would kill all the wild animals on Earth.

Artemis, the goddess of hunting, decided that Orion had to be stopped. She ordered a poisonous scorpion to go and sting him. Orion, who wasn't scared of the biggest animals,

An artist's interpretation of the constellation Orion the Hunter. Orion is most easily spotted in the night sky by his belt of three bright stars.

The night sky seen from Vancouver, Canada. In the centre-left you can see the belt of Orion (the three stars in a row). Off to the right is a tight cluster of seven stars called the Pleiades, representing seven sisters who were placed there to keep them safe from the pursuit of Orion.

did not even notice the tiny scorpion creeping from a hole in the ground. But then it stung him on his heel, and the giant dropped down dead.

This story is acted out above our heads in the night sky. Orion and the scorpion are both constellations. These are patterns of stars that were given the names of animals, gods and heroes by the ancient Greeks. Most of them look nothing like the things they are named after. However, the constellation known as Scorpio does look like a scorpion, and you can recognize Orion by his belt of three stars.

Orion is one of the brightest star groups in the northern winter sky. He is surrounded by other constellations showing hunting scenes. Facing him is the huge bull, Taurus, which Orion seems about to hit with his club.

This miniature painting from the sixteenth century shows a group of Arab astronomers in the Galata tower, in Constantinople.

Are constellations real?

To us, constellations look like fixed patterns of stars. But some of the stars are closer than others. So from a viewpoint somewhere else in space, the patterns they make would all be different.

The stars only seem to stay in the same positions because they are so far away.

In fact, they are moving at high speeds, often in different directions. The Great Bear, for example, has two stars which are moving in a different direction from the others. By the year 200,000 this constellation will look a different shape.

A thirteenth-century French astronomer studies the heavens.

This photo of the stars was taken over several hours. As the earth turned through the night, the stars appeared to move through the sky, leaving brilliantly coloured tracks of light behind them on the film. The stars are also moving in space.

Meanwhile his hunting dog, Canis Major, is chasing Lepus, the hare. The giant's hunt ends each spring, when the scorpion, creeping out of its hole, first rises in the eastern sky. Then Orion starts to fade away, sinking from view as if Scorpio had stung him.

What are constellations for?

People all over the world have always been fascinated by the stars. They have joined up the stars to make patterns and have told different stories about them. The Inuit of Alaska, for example, said that the stars of Orion's belt were three hunters, lost in the snow.

At first people studied the stars because they thought that they were gods, or that they controlled life on Earth in some way. Astrology, the idea that our lives are influenced by the constellations and the movements of the planets, is still very popular today.

Knowing about the stars proved to have many other uses. Because different constellations appear at different times of the year, they can be used like a calendar. This was very useful for early farmers. They knew that when a certain constellation appeared it was time for them to plant their crops.

Sailors discovered that the stars helped them to find their way at sea. They could find where north was by looking for the Pole Star, the star that lies directly above the North Pole. By measuring its height in the sky, they could also work out how far north or south their ship was.

Farming by the stars

Around 700 BC, a Greek writer called Hesiod wrote a poem for farmers: 'When Orion and Sirius come into mid-heaven, then set about cutting all the grape clusters… But when the mighty Orion is setting, then be thinking about ploughing.'

Christopher Columbus, back home after his voyage to the New World, checks his instruments. For many centuries, sailors like Columbus used the position of the stars as a way of plotting their course at night.

41

Globes of the stars

The ancient Greeks believed the sky was a solid, slowly turning ball, with the stars fixed on to it. This is what the night sky looks like. In fact, it is the Earth that is the spinning ball, not the sky.

Long before they built globes of the Earth, the Greeks made celestial (sky) globes. These showed the ball-shaped night sky as if viewed from outside. The constellations were all back to front.

Although we know that the sky isn't ball-shaped, this is still a useful way of mapping it. Like a globe of the Earth, a celestial globe can be divided up into lines of latitude and longitude, with an equator around the middle.

Above A celestial globe, made in 1584.

Right A map of the side of the Moon nearest to the Earth, from the *Encyclopaedia Londinensis* of 1802. It was based on observations made by Giovanni Riccioli and others.

Moon mapping

The clearest object in the night sky is the Moon. Since the 1600s, when telescopes were first used, people have been making maps of the Moon. They could only map one side of it. The Moon's far side is hidden from view.

If you look at the Moon, you can see that it has light and dark areas. The first people who mapped the Moon thought that the large, dark areas were seas.

In the 1650s, an Italian priest called Giovanni Riccioli, gave the different 'seas' names, such as the 'Sea of Showers' and the 'Ocean of Storms'. He also named craters and other features which he called bays, marshes and lakes. He used the names of famous people from history, as well as those of many of his own friends. We still use Riccioli's names today, even though we know that there are no seas on the Moon, just wide plains.

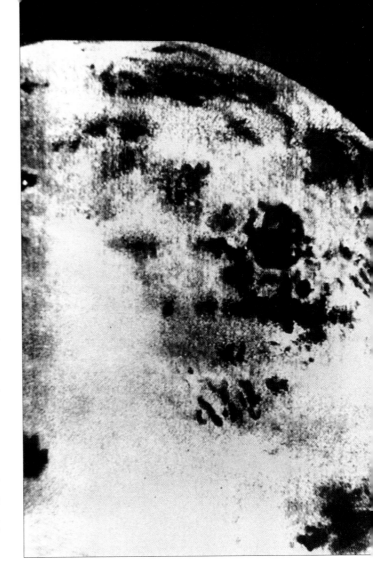

The first-ever photograph of the dark side of the Moon, taken in 1959 by the Russian *Luna 3* spacecraft. Until this photo was taken, no one knew for sure what was on the side of the Moon that faces away from the Earth.

The far side

In the 1960s, the USA and the USSR each launched spacecraft which circled the Moon, sending back photographs. At last, the mysterious far side could be seen and mapped. Hundreds of names had to be found for all of its newly discovered features.

Between 1967 and 1970, astronomers from the USA and the USSR held a series of meetings to decide on the names. They wanted to pay tribute to the people who had made flights to the Moon possible – the scientists, astronauts and cosmonauts.

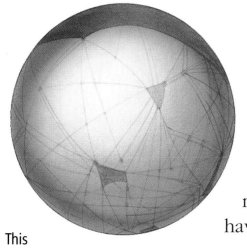

This picture is based on drawings of Mars made by Percival Lowell. The lines represent the canals which Lowell believed he could see on the planet's surface.

They also decided that the biggest features would be named after the most important people. Less important people would only have small craters named after them. There were many arguments about who deserved to have a place on the far side of the Moon.

The canals of Mars

Between 1894 and 1916, Mars was mapped in great detail by an American astronomer called Percival Lowell. Staring night after night at the red planet, he was convinced that he could see a network of lines crossing its surface. These lines looked so straight that he thought they must have been made by intelligent beings. Lowell called the lines 'canals' and began to draw maps of them.

Lowell could see from the lack of clouds that Mars was a very dry planet. He decided that the Martians must have built their huge canals to take water from the ice-caps at the poles to crops growing all over the planet.

Lowell's books and lectures on Mars caused great excitement. Millionaires offered prizes to anyone who could find a way to communicate with the Martians. Astronomy became a popular hobby.

In 1971, the US spacecraft *Mariner 9* surveyed Mars in great detail. It circled the planet twice a day for a whole year, sending back television pictures. However, it found no canals and no signs of life. The surface of Mars is an empty, red desert.

It seems that our eyes always look for patterns, even where they don't exist. We tend to join up scattered dark spots to form lines. The Martian canals had existed only in Percival Lowell's imagination.

A map of Mars made using a Mercator-style projection. It is easy to think you can see continents and oceans, because of the way in which the image has been coloured. In fact, the surface of Mars has no moisture and is utterly barren.

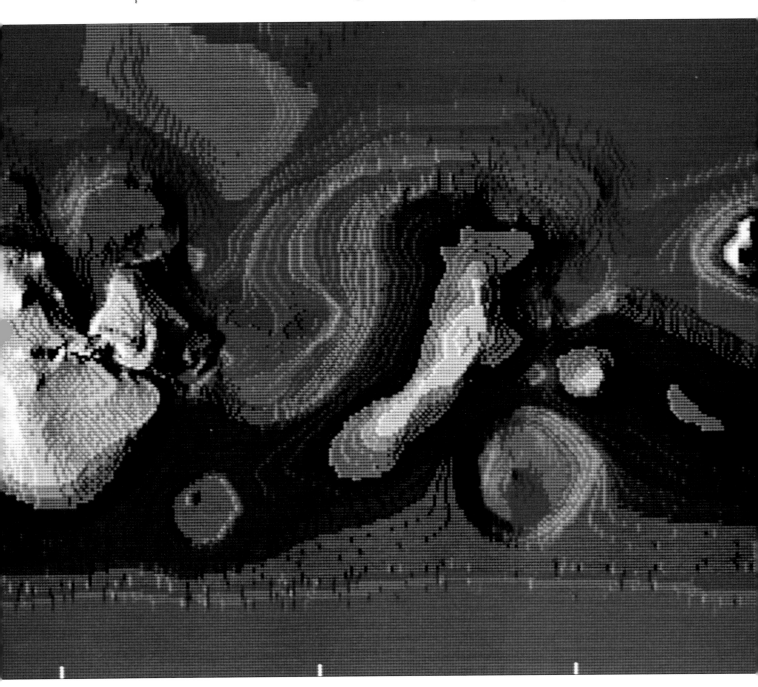

TIMELINE

c. 240 BC

Eratosthenes works out the size of the Earth by measuring a shadow cast by the sun

c. AD 150

Ptolemy explains how to make a map of the world, using lines of longitude and latitude

1492

Martin Behaim makes a globe of the Earth, the oldest still in existence. It doesn't show America. In the same year, Christopher Columbus crosses the Atlantic and 'discovers' the Americas

1543

Nicolas Copernicus argues that the Earth moves around the sun, rather than the other way around

1555–61

Philip Apian surveys Bavaria, using triangulation

1569

Gerhard Mercator publishes his map of the world

1609

The telescope invented in Holland

1687

Isaac Newton argues that the Earth is flatter at the poles than at the equator

1771

Contour lines first used, on a map of part of France

1850

First use of photography for mapping, from tall buildings, hot air balloons and kites

1872–76

The British ship *Challenger* explores the ocean floor

1912

Alfred Wegener argues that the different land-masses were once joined together

1931–33

Henry Beck produces his map of the London Underground

1959

Soviet spacecraft, *Luna 3*, sends back the first photographs of the far side of the Moon

1960

Jacques Picard and Donald Walsh reach the deepest point of the ocean bed, the bottom of the Pacific Marianas Trench, in a 'Bathyscape', or diving craft, called the *Trieste*

1960s

Electronic instruments for measuring distances begin to replace mapping by triangulation

GLOSSARY

Atlas A book of maps. Atlas was a giant who was believed to carry the world upon his shoulders. There was a picture of him on the title page of a 1595 book of maps by Gerhard Mercator. The book itself came to be called the 'Atlas'.

Constellation A group of stars that appear to fit together in a pattern

Contour lines Lines drawn on a map to show hills and valleys. They join together areas that are the same height above sea level.

Echo sounding (or Sonar) Using sound waves to measure the depth of water or detect underwater objects. A sound wave is sent to the bottom of the sea and the time it takes to echo back is recorded. Since the speed at which sound travels through water is known, the distance can be worked out.

Globe A ball-shaped model of the Earth or the sky

Latitude Position to the north or south of the Equator, an imaginary line drawn around the middle of the Earth. Lines of latitude are parallel to the Equator, and so they are known as 'parallels'.

Longitude Position to the east or west of an imaginary line drawn between the north and south poles. Lines of longitude are also known as 'meridians'.

Projection A way of showing our round Earth on a flat piece of paper

Scale The difference between distances on a map and in the real world

Sphere A ball-shaped object

Survey Measurement of the exact position of places

Topographical maps Maps that show features of a landscape, such as hills, valleys and rivers

Triangulation A method of surveying a country by plotting triangles

FURTHER INFORMATION

BOOKS

Tales from the Map Room by Peter Barber and Christopher Board (BBC Books, 1993) Although this is for adults, it is worth finding for the beautiful illustrations. It looks at many different kinds of map.

How to Draw Maps and Charts by Pam Beasant and Alastair Smith (Usborne, 1993)

Maps and Mapping by Barbara Taylor (Kingfisher Young Discoverers, 1992)

Planet Earth; a Visual Factfinder by Michael Allenby and Neil Curtis (Kingfisher, 1993)

The Oceans Atlas by Anita Ganeri (Dorling Kindersley, 1994)

Seas and Oceans by David Lambert (Watts, 1992)

Exploring the Sea by Daniel Rogers (Wayland, 1991)

The Space Atlas by Ian Nicholson (Oxford, 1992)

CD-ROM

Small Blue Planet (Now What Software, 1994) A satellite's-eye view of the Earth.

INDEX